STORIES
of the SAINTS

JOYCE DENHAM

ILLUSTRATED BY
JUDY STEVENS

PARACLETE PRESS
BREWSTER, MASSACHUSETTS

For Saints David and Irene,
parents in faith J.D.

For Chris J.S.

Stories of the Saints

2007 First Printing this Edition
Text copyright © 2001 Joyce Denham
Illustrations copyright © 2001 Judy Stevens
This edition copyright © 2003 Lion Publishing

ISBN 13: 978-1-55725-534-1

Published in the United States
by **Paraclete Press**, 2007.
Originally published in 2001, 2003 by
Lion Publishing plc
Mayfield House, 256 Banbury Road,
Oxford OX2 7DH, England

3 5 7 9 10 8 6 4 2

Acknowledgments
Scripture quotations on pp. 5, 7 (Luke 1:46–48), 8 (Isaiah 7:14), 10 (Luke 1:76), 19, 24
(Ephesians 3:18) are taken from the *Holy Bible* New Living Translation, copyright © 1996.
Used by permission of Tyndale House Publishers, Inc., Wheaton, Illinois 60189. All rights reserved.
(The above translation was the author's main Bible reference when preparing this book.)
Scripture quotation on p. 25 quoted from the Good News Bible published by
The Bible Societies/HarperCollins Publishers Ltd, UK © American Bible Society
1966, 1971, 1976, 1992, used with permission.

Published by Paraclete Press
Brewster, Massachusetts
www.paracletepress.com

Printed and bound in Singapore

CONTENTS

INTRODUCTION

This book tells the stories of fourteen saints who lived long ago. They were, in many ways, ordinary humans just like each of us. But they had one thing in common: They loved God more than anything else in the world. And they tried to show God's love to everyone they met—even if it ruffled feathers and made people angry; even if people laughed at them for it.

Their love for God filled them with faith and courage. They stood up to Kings and Queens and entire armies, all for the sake of speaking the truth: God's truth, rooted in self-sacrificing love and forgiveness. And because their hearts were so open to God, God loved and spoke and moved through them.

Saints are, quite simply, people who are in love with God and follow God no matter what it costs. They exist in every place and time.

In the first section of this book, *God with Us*, you'll meet four saints—two men and two women—who were very much involved in the greatest event in human history: the birth and life of Jesus, through whom God visited our earth as a man. Through his life, death, and resurrection, Jesus showed the whole world how much God loves us.

The next section, *A New Kingdom*, tells of two saints who helped to establish Jesus' church—the family of his followers in every generation.

Finally, in *The Light Shines in the Darkness*, you'll meet eight more saints, from many different countries, who—centuries after Jesus ascended back to heaven—continued to carry the light of God's love into a dark and hurting world. For some, it cost them their lives.

O come, O come, Immanuel,
And ransom captive Israel,
That mourns in lonely exile here,
Until the Son of God appear.
Rejoice! Rejoice! Immanuel
Shall come to thee, O Israel.

(Twelfth-century Advent hymn)

GOD WITH US

Look! The virgin will conceive a child!
She will give birth to a son and will
call him Immanuel – 'God is with us.'

Isaiah 7:14

MARY

'I am the Lord's Servant.'

Young Mary gasped in fear.

A splendid angel stood before her and was clearly speaking: 'Greetings! The Lord is with you!'

Mary shrank from the dazzling presence.

'Do not fear, Mary,' the angel said. 'God has called you blessed! You will bear a child and will name him Jesus. He will be the Son of the Most High. He will sit on the throne of King David, your ancestor, and he will reign for ever and ever!'

'But how can this thing be?' Mary stammered. 'I will not sleep with a man until I am married. How can I have a child?'

Stretching himself forth, the magnificent being announced: 'The Holy Spirit will come upon you. The power of God, the Most High, will overshadow you. Your holy child will be the Son of God.

'Your cousin Elizabeth will also bear a son – even though she is an old woman. For with God, nothing is impossible!'

Mary fell on her knees – for she knew that the visitor was God's own messenger – and she felt the doors of her heart open wide. Her voice came strong and clear.

'I am the Lord's servant!' she shouted joyously. 'Whatever God asks me to do, I will surely do!' And she raised her hands to heaven.

Then the angel vanished, and Mary was alone, filled with joy and wonder.

Soon afterwards, Mary set out to visit her elderly cousin. When Elizabeth saw Mary approaching her home, she felt her own baby jump inside her.

'It is an honour to be visited by the mother of my Lord!' she cried.

Falling into each other's arms, they laughed in amazement; and Mary threw back her head and sang this song:

'Oh, how I praise the Lord.
How I rejoice in God my Saviour!
For he took notice of his lowly servant girl,
and now generation after generation will
call me blessed.'

However, when she returned to her parents' home in Nazareth, trouble waited. Her fiancé, Joseph, heard that she was pregnant. It was whispered that he planned to break off their engagement. The women she met by the village well as she filled her water jar eyed her with pity and scorn. Mary hung her head: what was Joseph meant to do? How could he marry her when she was already pregnant with a child – and he was not the father?

She was walking home from the well, her mind lost in troubled thoughts, when suddenly someone grabbed her, knocking the clay pot from her arms, spilling water everywhere. It was Joseph!

'Mary,' he pleaded, 'you will still marry me, won't you? Can you forgive me? I was so angry and afraid. But last night, while I was sleeping, I was visited in a dream by…'

'An angel?'

'It was Gabriel!' said Joseph. 'He told me not to be afraid; and that I should take you as my wife because the baby in your womb is holy, the child of God's Spirit; we are to name the child – '

'Yes, I know,' Mary said quickly. 'We are to name him Jesus!'

'It means "The Lord Saves"! This child will save our people from their sins. Mary, you are to be the mother of the Messiah – the Saviour promised so long ago.'

'My cousin, Elizabeth, is pregnant too!' Mary added. 'She's past the sixth month!'

'It's impossible!' Joseph exclaimed. 'She's too old!'

'But it's true! Some time ago, the angel Gabriel also visited Elizabeth's husband, Zechariah.'

'But why them? What were they told?'

'That their prayers for a family are answered and that Elizabeth's son will prepare the way for the Messiah!'

'And then,' said Joseph excitedly, putting it all together, 'the angel visited each of us saying that you will be the *mother* of the Messiah!'

He took her hands in his.

'Great prophecies are coming true, Mary. We must do whatever God commands us!'

Some months later, Mary and Joseph travelled to Bethlehem – the ancient city of their ancestor, King David – so they could be counted in the census, which was being taken throughout the entire Roman Empire.

When they arrived in Bethlehem, it was time for Mary to have her baby. But the city was crowded because of the census and all the inns were full. The only place Joseph could find for Mary was a little cave, used as an animal shelter. Here it was that she gave birth to Jesus.

Late that same night, outside the bustling town, there were shepherds in the fields, quietly watching over their sheep. Suddenly, a magnificent light burst into the sky above them, blazing like a great fire.

The shepherds fell back in terror.

'Don't be afraid!' a voice resounded. 'I am bringing you news of great joy! Tonight, in Bethlehem – the city of David – your Saviour, the Messiah, is born. Go: you will find him lying in a manger!'

Then the angel was joined by a great choir of angels singing together: 'Glory to God in the highest heaven, and peace on earth to everyone who pleases God!'

Instantly, the sky was swallowed in darkness; and without stopping to think, the shepherds abandoned their flocks and hurried towards the city to find the Messiah. Their search brought them to the edge of town, to a rough cave at the foot of a low and rocky hill. There they found Mary and Joseph and Jesus, just as the angel had said.

The weary shepherds fell on their knees and sang out, 'At last! The Saviour of Israel is here!'

In the morning, burning with excitement, they danced through the winding streets of Bethlehem – up one alleyway and down another – telling everyone about what they had seen and heard: 'Our king is born!' they shouted. 'We have seen the Messiah, the Saviour of Israel! Go and see him for yourselves!'

The people looked at each other amazed.

'Who is this new king they speak of?'

'Have they gone mad?'

'What is the meaning of this uproar?'

But Mary knew its meaning. Even as a tiny child, she had learned the words of the ancient prophet Isaiah, and she had learned to hope in them, as all her people had done. Now, as she tenderly cradled her baby, she repeated them over and over in her heart:

Look! The virgin will conceive a child!
She will give birth to a son and will
call him Immanuel – 'God is with us.'

JOHN THE BAPTIST

(First century, Judea)

'I am a voice shouting in the wilderness.'

People wondered about Jesus' cousin John.

What was he doing, living alone in the wilderness, eating locusts and honey and dressing in rough shirts woven from camel hair?

Occasionally, people walking to the next town caught glimpses of him.

'He was sun-scorched and wild-looking!' they said.

'I heard him howl!'

'He runs over the hills like a jackal!'

His parents, Elizabeth and Zechariah, were wounded by these reports. They often asked themselves what it had meant when, thirty years earlier, Zechariah had prophesied at John's birth:

'And you, my little son,
will be called the prophet of the Most High,
because you will prepare the way for the Lord.'

Then one day travellers came, telling everyone about a holy man shouting in the desert: 'Make a path for the Lord's coming! Make the road straight before him!'

Throughout the region people came with stories of the man shouting in the desert: 'Turn from your sins! Turn your hearts to God! The kingdom of heaven is near!'

People from Jerusalem and the entire Jordan Valley streamed into the wilderness to hear John preach; and when they confessed their sins, he baptized them in the River Jordan dipping them under the dark, eddying water and lifting them up into the bright sunlight.

But to some people his message was harsh.

'You snakes!' he shouted to those he knew were not truly repentant. 'Why are you coming to be baptized when you are only pretending to be sorry for your sins? You think you are religious, but you still do wrong to your neighbour. Prove that you really intend to follow God!'

'What must we do?' people asked.

'If you have two coats,' said John, 'give one to someone who is poor. If you have food, share it with the hungry.'

The cheating tax collectors asked what they should do. 'Be honest,' he said. 'Collect only the taxes that Rome requires.'

The scheming soldiers asked what they should do. 'Stop accusing people of crimes they did not commit,' he told them. 'And stop forcing people to give you their money.'

Everyone was hungry for his message. Thousands of people waded into the River Jordan when they realized how far they had failed. They came out of the river ready to start anew.

They asked themselves: could John be the

Messiah, the one chosen by God to save his people? Or the prophet Elijah, come back from the dead?

John answered them: 'I am only a voice shouting in the wilderness. I have come to baptize you with water, but someone else is coming who will baptize you with the Holy Spirit!'

At last, Elizabeth and Zechariah understood. Centuries earlier the prophet Isaiah had spoken of a messenger: 'He will be a voice crying in the wilderness: "Prepare a way for the Lord!" '

Their own son, John the Baptist, was that messenger.

Then the day came when John's cousin Jesus – the carpenter from Nazareth – asked John to baptize him.

'No!' John protested, for he knew who Jesus was and the way he lived. 'You should be baptizing me!'

Jesus insisted. And when Jesus came up out of the water, John saw the Holy Spirit – in the shape of a dove – come down from heaven and descend on Jesus.

This was the moment John was waiting for, and now he knew for certain that his cousin Jesus was the Messiah.

'Here is the one who takes away the sins of the world!' he shouted excitedly. 'Here is the one who will baptize you with the Holy Spirit!' And then he declared to all the people that Jesus was the Son of God.

PETER

'Lord, save me!'

Peter had a habit of jumping into the sea.

The first time was extremely risky, downright foolhardy, his friends thought. They were crammed into one of Peter's small fishing boats, all twelve of Jesus' disciples. It was dark and they were exhausted. All day, thousands of people had been following Jesus, begging him to heal their children, asking him to preach, hanging on his every word.

'You must rest,' Jesus had told the twelve. 'Jump into the boat and get away while I send the crowds home.'

They knew it would take hours to cross the huge lake, even longer now that the wind had turned against them. As the night wore on the men grew nervous: the air smelled of danger; the sea was stirring. At about three in the morning, the storm broke hard upon them. High into the air the seething waters heaved their boat; it teetered on the crest of the wave, then plunged into the deep trough.

'We're going to die!' they shouted in terror.

'What's that?' screamed Andrew, as a human figure appeared before them on the water.

'It's a spirit!' the men cried in horror. 'We're doomed!'

But the 'spirit' assured them: 'Don't fear!' it said. 'I'm here! You're safe now!'

Is it true? thought Peter. Dare I believe that Jesus has come to us on the sea?

'Lord,' he called, 'if it's truly you, let me walk to you on the water!'

'Come!' Jesus replied, beckoning.

Instantly Peter was over the side of the boat, walking on the water! Running on the water! But the waves were so huge. He looked around in terror – and then he was sinking, gasping for breath. 'Lord, save me!' he cried.

Jesus grabbed him with strong arms and pulled him up. 'What happened to your faith?' he asked. 'What made you start doubting?'

They climbed into the boat. At once the sea was calm, and Peter looked at Jesus in amazement. 'Truly you are the Son of God!' he said. Never again would he doubt his Lord, he told himself. Never again would he give in to fear, no matter how terrifying the events.

After that, Peter's faith was firm: he had left everything to follow Jesus. The other disciples admired his boldness, his passion for God's truth, his reckless devotion to the Lord.

Then everything changed. That night when they were all together, eating the Passover supper, Jesus himself said those shocking words: 'One of you will betray me to the authorities tonight. I will be arrested, and all of you will desert me.'

Peter broke the stunned silence. 'No, Lord! Not me! I will never desert you!'

'Oh, Peter,' Jesus had answered him, 'if only I could spare you from what is to come. Satan, the evil one, will fight for your soul tonight. But I am praying for you. And when you turn back to me, I want you to strengthen your fellow believers.'

'No, Lord,' Peter had protested. 'Even if the

others give in to fear and forsake you, I never will.'

'Ah,' said Jesus, 'before the cock crows twice in the early dawn, you will have denied me three times.'

'I will never deny you!' Peter had vowed. 'I will die for you if I have to!'

So what was the new feeling of fear that swept over him as later that night he waited, sick with anxiety, outside the home of the high priest?

After the Passover supper, they had gone to a quiet garden where Jesus could be alone to pray. Never had Peter seen him so troubled. The next thing he knew there was a terrible commotion. (How could I have fallen asleep? he thought with dismay.) There were Roman soldiers everywhere – and officers from the temple, even the chief priests and elders! Swords drawn! Torches blazing in the night! Swiftly the men seized Jesus and bound him.

Into the dark night the disciples fled. But as the guards led Jesus away, Peter followed. He slipped silently between buildings, moved in and out of the shadows, then ever so slyly found a place at the campfire in the courtyard of the high priest's residence – where they were questioning Jesus. He stood among the servants, trying to look like one of them; but a nagging fear, like a snake, slithered into his soul.

The fire leaped and danced. One of the servant girls was staring at him. 'You're one of his followers, aren't you?' she said.

His palms sweated; his heart pounded. 'No, I'm not!' he was saying. 'I don't know the man!'

'Yes you do!' the other servants joined in. 'Your accent gives you away – you sound like a Galilean!'

Waves of fear towered over him. 'I'm telling you, I've never met him!'

'You're one of them!' the guards shouted. 'One of his disciples!'

The sea of terror broke over him, choking him, sucking him under.

'No! I do not know him!' he growled.

The shrill scream of the cock broke the shadowy dawn, once, twice. Oh, Lord! he cried in his heart. How can you save me now? And he fled the scene, the burning tears streaming down his face.

The next day, Jesus was crucified, nailed to a cross of wood while his friends stood at a distance. After his body was buried, the disciples stayed in hiding. When some women went back to the tomb, they claimed that the body had gone and that Jesus had risen from the dead. Peter thought they had lost their senses. Then Jesus appeared to several of them. So it was true! But Peter felt more lost than ever, like being alone on a drifting ship, looking for others to help him to shore.

Later, Peter and the others were back in Galilee. They went out in Peter's boat, wondering what would happen next. All night they fished and caught nothing. They were so discouraged.

In the early dawn a man called to them from the shore. 'Did you find fish?' he asked.

'No!' they shouted.

'Then put your net down on the other side of the boat!'

Something made them obey the stranger. Suddenly they caught so many fish they wondered if they could haul them to shore.

Then Peter realized who the man was: Jesus, the Lord. He leaped from the boat into the cold

water, and swam to shore – where Jesus was waiting for them, cooking breakfast over a fire. Soon they all ate their fill, singing and laughing with delight.

After this, Peter's faith never wavered. For the rest of his life he spoke boldly, encouraging those who believed in Jesus. He gave his life to spread the news Jesus brought – that love can conquer evil – and to pass on Jesus' promise of a new life, free from the fear of death.

A day came when Peter, too, was seized by Roman soldiers and put on trial for his faith. But Jesus had prayed for him. Even when his executioners came to do their worst, he stood firm. Billows of pain broke over his head. Seas of fear swept under him. 'Lord, save me!' he cried victoriously, and he didn't sink.

MARY MAGDALENE

(FIRST CENTURY, GALILEE)

'I have seen the Lord!'

It was Sunday morning, very early.

In the still blackness before dawn Mary made her way to the tomb of Jesus. She turned and whispered to her companions, 'Quietly! There are Roman soldiers guarding the tomb!'

On Friday night, after Jesus was crucified, they had laid his body in the cave and the guards had sealed the opening with a huge stone. Now the women were coming to anoint their Lord's body with spices.

They crept into the graveyard and peered anxiously towards the tomb. The stone was gone! The Roman guards were not there! Instead, alone in the darkness, stood a young man, bathed in light, at the door to the tomb.

He was speaking. 'Why are you looking for Jesus of Nazareth in a graveyard?' he asked. 'He's alive! He has risen from the dead!'

The women ran back to Jerusalem to tell their friends. But Mary was puzzled: who was this stranger? What did the words mean? How could anyone believe Jesus was alive again? Her thoughts raced. Where had the young man vanished to? Was he an angel? Or was it a trick? Had the authorities stolen Jesus' body so that she couldn't embalm it properly?

Alone in the early dawn, she returned to the tomb, weeping.

If only Jesus had been more cautious and hadn't angered the Jewish priests and rulers. Despite his healing miracles, they suspected him. 'He claims to be God!' some of them had shouted in outrage. 'No one who makes himself equal with God deserves to live! He must be put to death!'

As she watched him die the previous Friday, nailed to a Roman cross like a common criminal, she had felt such anguish. Three years earlier, Jesus had ordered seven evil spirits to leave her and she had felt free and at peace, but now she felt herself sinking under the force of old fears – voices in her head told her she was ugly and worthless, unfit to live. Bitter blackness crept into her soul, like a cat on the hunt, crouching and sneaking and pouncing.

'If only Jesus hadn't left us!' she sobbed aloud. 'I thought he was the Messiah, the Saviour of Israel!'

She froze. Someone was behind her. Was it a soldier come to seize her too?

'Oh!' she gasped in relief as she turned and saw the gardener.

'Why are you weeping?' he asked.

'Because someone has stolen the body that was buried here – the body of Jesus. If you know who took him or where they put him, please tell me!' she pleaded.

He answered her with such overwhelming tenderness: 'Mary!'

Then she knew him, just as surely as he knew her: it was Jesus! At that moment, the sun burst over the horizon, gold and crimson, piercing the darkness in her heart, shattering her fears, lighting up the whole world.

'Teacher!' she shouted in a burst of pure joy.

'Run quickly, Mary, and tell Peter and the others that you have seen me – that I have risen from the dead, just as I said I would! Tell them to go immediately to Galilee and I will meet them there!'

Mary almost knocked down the door of the house where the disciples were hiding as she ran in shouting, 'I have seen the Lord!'

In the days that followed, before Jesus ascended to heaven, he told his disciples to spread this good news: Christ has conquered death! The way to God is opened!

All over the world they travelled, telling everyone they met that Jesus had risen from the dead – and that the first person to see him had been Mary Magdalene.

Love's redeeming work is done;
Fought the fight, the battle won…
Death in vain forbids his rise;
Christ has opened Paradise.
Charles Wesley

A NEW KINGDOM

The kingdom of heaven is like a treasure
that a man discovered hidden in a field.
In his excitement, he hid it again and sold
everything he owned to get enough money
to buy the field – and to get the treasure, too!
Matthew 13:44

STEPHEN

(FIRST CENTURY, JERUSALEM)

'I can see the heavens opened!'

Trouble was brewing in Jerusalem.

The Jewish authorities thought that once Jesus was dead his followers would give up, but Peter and the others stood daily at the gates of the Jewish Temple, preaching in loud voices: 'Jesus of Nazareth was raised from the dead! He is the true Messiah of Israel. He has brought the kingdom of God to earth!' Thousands and thousands of people joined the disciples as followers of Jesus the Christ.

These believers, as they were called, gathered at the Temple in crowds, worshipping together. They were so full of love for God, their hearts spilled over with generosity. People listening to them heard the most amazing things: 'I have an extra cloak, you take it!'; 'We have extra food; your family can eat it,' and 'I'll sell my house and everyone can share in the profits.' The word spread all over town: among the believers there was no poverty.

What's more, the believers made it clear that they were citizens of a new kingdom – God's kingdom. The jealousy of the Jewish judges erupted: 'We must stop them!' they agreed.

But Gamaliel, a much respected teacher of the Jewish law, convinced the judges to let the disciples be. 'If what they teach is not from God,' he reasoned, 'their plans will come to nothing. But if God is behind them, you can do nothing to stop them.'

All went well until men from the Synagogue of Freed Slaves decided to argue with Stephen, one of seven deacons who organized the daily life of the new church – the community of Jesus' followers.

'Let's catch him in a debate,' the schemers said. 'He's bound to say something illegal, and then we'll take him to court!'

But they were no match for Stephen. They questioned and goaded him – but Stephen answered wisely. They needled and cajoled him – but Stephen so baffled them with his knowledge, the men looked foolish. 'We'll trick him!' they decided. Secretly, they hired several swindlers to go before the Jewish High Council and say that Stephen had broken the law by speaking against God and their ancestor Moses. He was arrested on the spot and put on trial.

The 'witnesses' stood before the high priest and lied. 'This man keeps saying that Jesus will destroy our Temple, and the whole law of Moses!' they shouted.

Suddenly, everyone stared at Stephen, their mouths open: his face looked like an angel's face.

Regaining their composure, the priests confronted him. 'Is this true?' they asked.

Stephen did not answer their question. Instead, he began to retell the entire history of Israel – how God called Abraham and Sarah and made from them a great nation; how through the centuries God sent prophets to tell his people of the Messiah who would some day bring the kingdom of God to earth. 'Your ancestors killed the prophets,' he declared, 'and now you have killed the Messiah!'

The priests were furious, but Stephen was

unmoved. 'Look!' he cried as he gazed upward. 'I can see the heavens opened and Jesus standing next to God's right hand!'

'Enough!' they screamed, and they rushed at him, covering their ears and shouting to drown out his voice. Outside the gates of the city they dragged him, where they fell on him and hurled stones at his head. An eager young man named Saul held the murderer's cloaks and cheered them on.

'Oh, Lord!' Stephen cried. 'Take me to heaven now. And don't blame these people for this sin!' And then he died. He was the first believer to give up his life rather than renounce his faith in Jesus.

PAUL

(First century, Jerusalem)

'By God's love, I can see!'

The Jews in Damascus could hardly believe their ears.

For there was Saul of Tarsus, the chief enemy of the followers of Jesus, standing in the synagogue shouting, 'Jesus of Nazareth is the Son of God!'

Swiftly, the leaders of the synagogues met in council. 'Two weeks ago,' one of them said, 'we had word from the chief priests in Jerusalem, that we were to help Saul arrest Jesus' followers. Yet now he arrives preaching that Jesus is the Son of God! What are we to make of it?'

'He is playing tricks on us,' said another. 'We know how crafty he is, and if he no longer wants to kill the followers of Jesus – perhaps he now wants to kill us!'

They agreed together, 'We will be cautious and watch everything he does.'

Meanwhile, Jesus' followers in Damascus already knew the truth about Saul. Several days earlier they had been meeting in secret when they heard that Saul was on his way to Damascus, and that he had been given authority by the high priest in Jerusalem to arrest them, put them in chains, and take them to Jerusalem to be tried.

As they discussed what to do, Ananias – one of their group – came in, shouting, 'Friends! God has chosen Saul of Tarsus to carry the message of Jesus to the Gentiles! He is filled with the Holy Spirit, just as we are.'

'What do you mean?' they cried in alarm.

Then they all scrambled back in fear as Saul entered the room. Children hid behind their parents; parents exchanged looks; heads nodded ever so slightly toward the windows, indicating ways of escape.

'My dear fellow believers!' Saul began.

They gasped.

'You have reason to be afraid of me. When Stephen was killed in Jerusalem, I held his murderers' cloaks; I hunted Jesus' followers, pulling them from their homes in the night; I had them arrested. In fact, I was on my way to Damascus to arrest all of you!

'But listen,' Saul continued. 'Several days ago, as I was travelling to your city, a fierce light from heaven blinded me. I fell to my knees in the road and heard a voice calling my name: "Saul! Saul!" it said. "Why are you persecuting me?"

' "Who are you?" I cried out in terror.

' "I am Jesus," the voice answered, "the one you are persecuting!"

'Then my companions led me, blind and shaking with fear, to a lodging here in Damascus, where for three days I ate and drank nothing, stumbling about in utter blackness, my sight gone.

'I prayed fervently to God. And one by one, the ancient prophecies about the Jewish Messiah came to my mind. I was astounded – Jesus of Nazareth fulfilled them all! I suddenly knew that he is the Christ, the promised Saviour. Although my eyes were darkened, my heart was full of light. I saw the truth! And I saw how evil was my hatred of the believers. Now I, too, yearned to follow Jesus, but what was I to do?

'Just then, Ananias knocked at my door. The Lord had sent him, and when he laid hands on me and prayed, callouses fell from my eyes – I could see again! Ananias baptized me. And now I intend to enter every synagogue in Damascus, preaching the truth about Jesus the Christ.'

The believers sat spellbound. At first they talked quietly, then excitedly, then joyfully! Soon they were embracing Saul and praising God together.

'God has forgiven him!' one of them declared. 'And so must we!'

Saul did exactly as he said. He went daily into all the synagogues in Damascus and preached to the Jews, saying that Jesus was the Son of God.

As the number of new believers grew and grew, the leaders of the synagogues began to hate Saul. They felt he had betrayed them and now they wanted him dead.

One evening as Saul met with some of his followers, a young girl burst into the room. 'They are plotting to kill Saul!' she exclaimed. 'I heard it said by someone leaving the synagogue. Spies are watching each of the city gates!'

They waited for a dark night when the moon

had waned; and taking Saul, a few of them set out into the narrow, winding streets of Damascus. They moved silently, keeping behind the buildings, moving in the shadows, until they reached the city wall.

In the blackness, high above them, Saul could just detect a gaping hole in the stonework. They fastened a basket – one with long, long ropes knotted securely to its rim – to Saul's back, leaving the ropes to dangle freely behind him.

No one uttered a word but, with tears streaming down their faces, they hugged him long and hard. Then up the wall he climbed, slowly, inch-by-inch, until he had reached the gap. He took the basket from his back and pushed it through the hole, while his friends below grabbed the ends of their attached ropes and held tight. The basket hung just below the gap, on the other side of the wall.

Saul's feet were last to disappear as he wriggled through the hole himself. Then the ropes went taut, and the men held on even tighter, as Saul dropped into the waiting basket. Bit by bit, they let out their lines, gently lowering Saul to the

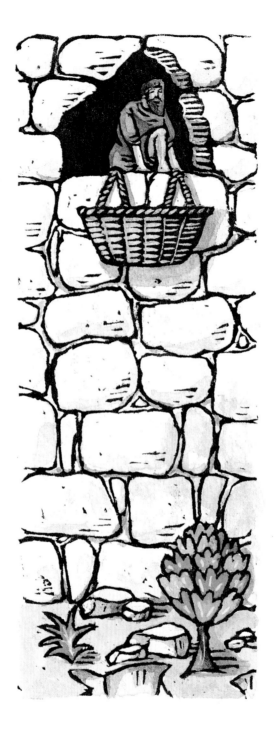

ground on the other side. He was alone in the darkness outside the city wall. He was safe.

Saul spent the rest of his life spreading the Good News of Christ all over the Roman world. He was a Jew, but he devoted a great deal of his time to helping the Gentiles – the non-Jews – frequently risking his life to tell them that Jesus was their Messiah too.

In time, Saul became known by the Gentile version of his name: Paul. With Paul's help, the Jewish and Gentile believers in Jesus put away their differences. They all followed one Lord, and soon they were all called by one name: Christians – followers of the Christ.

Paul wanted all Christians to be united in love. And if anyone knew what it was like to receive God's love, it was Paul. God had forgiven him all his murderous deeds, and Paul never forgot that. To his friends in the city of Ephesus he wrote:

'May you have the power to understand, as all God's people should, how wide, how long, how high, and how deep his love really is.'

Wide enough and deep enough to reach Saul of Tarsus.

O come, thou Dayspring, come and cheer
Our spirits by thine advent here;
And drive away the shades of night,
And pierce the clouds and bring us light!
(Twelfth-century Advent hymn)

THE LIGHT SHINES
IN THE DARKNESS

… and the darkness
has never put it out.
John 1:5

LAURENCE

(THIRD CENTURY, ROME)

'I will show you the treasures of the church.'

Laurence knew he had only three days to live.

But death would bring an end to the living nightmare he had witnessed that morning.

They had gathered in the cemetery of Praetextatus – he and his fellow-Christians who were bold enough to worship in public. They had come to hear their leader, Pope Sixtus, speak.

'Beloved brothers and sisters,' Sixtus began. 'As you know, the Roman emperor, Valerian, despises Christianity. Now he has commanded

that, on penalty of death, all the people who hold positions of responsibility in our community must offer sacrifices to the pagan gods of Rome.

'Such a thing we will never do! We worship the one true Lord, Jesus the Christ, who at our deaths will crown us with life eternal –'

At that moment, a band of Roman soldiers, swords drawn, rushed over the hill and seized him. 'This is what you get for refusing to obey the emperor!' they taunted, and they slew him with their swords.

Laurence looked on, stupefied. His beloved master lay dead. And as the Pope's archdeacon, he would be next.

'You! You are his servant,' a soldier said gruffly, grabbing Laurence. They marched him to the palace, then forced him to his knees before the Roman prefect.

'You Christ-worshipping swine!' the prefect sneered. 'Sixtus gave you charge of the community's books and records, and all the gold and valuables of what you call your church – is this not true?'

'It is,' Laurence answered boldly, 'but I use the gold to provide for the needy among us.'

'The wealth of your church belongs to the emperor!' the prefect roared. 'You will bring it to me at once.'

'But it will take days,' Laurence protested.

'You will bring me the treasures of the church in three days,' the prefect warned, 'or you, too, shall die!'

Quickly Laurence returned to the church

building. He filled hundreds of small sacks with the gold that was kept there. Then he sent his workers to the market to sell the church's fabrics, plates and cups. Then they filled more sacks with the gold from the sales.

When the sun set, they delivered the little sacks to poor people all over Rome. 'Use this gold to buy food,' they whispered, 'and when we send the word, come to the church building with haste!'

After three days, it was all ready.

Laurence walked valiantly to see the prefect. 'Come to the church,' he said. 'I have gathered all our wealth.'

When the prefect arrived, he was stunned and repulsed by what he saw: people with festering sores, blind eyes, broken backs, missing limbs, unwashed bodies, tattered rags for clothes.

'Here they are,' Laurence said, opening his loving arms to the crowd, 'the treasures of the church!'

In a fury, the prefect struck Laurence and dragged him to the executioner. 'I want him dead by sunset!' he cried.

Laurence's death brought new life to the struggling church in Rome. Instead of growing weaker, the Christians grew stronger. Laurence's boldness inspired them, and as they preached the words of Christ, more and more treasures were added to the church.

MARTIN OF TOURS

(FOURTH CENTURY, FRANCE)

'Often, often, often goes the Christ in the stranger's guise.'

(Ancient Celtic Rune)

It was a bitter winter in France.

Martin – a young soldier in the Roman army at Amiens – was helping to hold these lands for the empire: he had quashed rebellions and invasions, quelled riots, and fought for the peace of Rome. He was bone-cold and sick of killing.

During the easy times, when things were quiet, he paced endlessly at his post, stiff from shivering, the cold stinging his eyes. His cloak offered some comfort: it was his only defence against the icy blasts. But he had lived in the

thing for months, and now it stank.

During the hard times he had become ruthless, brutal. He beat rebels and their families, tortured them, even killed them with his own hands. When barbarians crossed the borders, he was proud to be part of the army and he helped to slaughter them by the hundreds. Martin had so much blood on his hands, he was sickened by his own life.

'The Christians refuse to fight,' his comrade said to him one day, as they shivered at their post.

'Hmph!' Martin scoffed. 'All that talk about loving their enemies – where would Rome be today if we all did that?' As he spoke, his breath froze in the cold air.

'The Christians are cowards, afraid to fight!' the other soldier replied.

Martin wrapped his cloak about him more tightly, because (despite his brave words) with each battle he fought for Rome, he fought a fiercer battle inside his own heart. Many were the times he had actually thought of severing himself from the soldier's ugly duties, but a bitter white frost had settled over the landscape of his soul.

Secretly, he admired the Christians. Certainly it took greater strength to love your enemies than to destroy them – a thing anyone could do. For centuries now the Christians had willingly died for their beliefs: nailed to crosses, or thrown into circus rings to be mauled by wild beasts, they faced death unflinchingly. Their spirit was unconquerable; their way of love and forgiveness was full of power. Dared he leave the army and follow their God?

No, that would take far more courage than he

possessed. He felt tortured by violence and hate, it was true; but if he refused to fight, he would be imprisoned – quite possibly killed.

At nightfall, relieved of his watch, he hurried back to camp. The moon bathed the road before him in a chill white light. He pressed forward, leaning into the wind as the night's icy breath blew across his face and tugged at his cloak.

He stopped at the sound of a lonely, awful moan. His breath whistled; his heart thumped.

Nothing. It must have been the wind.

There it was again, louder now.

'Who's calling?' he cried, whirling round.

'It is I, sir!' a voice whined.

'What are you doing out here, man?' Martin bellowed, nearly stumbling over a shivering, half-naked peasant crouched by the roadside. 'The night is bitter! You'll die by morning!'

'Sir, I have nowhere to go – no blankets and no food, nowhere even to lay my head! Can you help me?' asked the man feebly.

'Can I help you? I am a soldier. Now leave this road at once or I shall arrest you!' And Martin turned and marched on.

But the battle inside Martin's soul flared. What if the man froze to death? What if no one took pity? What would it be like to die all alone in the cold night?

Martin pulled his cloak in tighter. How foolish the old man was – to be out on such a night with no covering, hoping someone else would take care of him. I'm here to keep order, he thought; I can't be encouraging beggars. Besides, he might try to steal my cloak.

Then it struck him: he was the same as this lonely beggar. In fact, his cloak was their only difference. 'Without it, I, too, would freeze,' he said aloud. 'I, too, am lost and afraid – only on the inside.'

Suddenly, courage sprang up inside his heart, and he turned and ran back to the old man.

'Wait!' he shouted. 'I can indeed help you!' His sword glinted in the moonlight as Martin cut the cloak in two and gave half to the stranger. Then he ran all the way to camp with his half-cloak thrown across his back.

Later that night, as he dozed by the fire, a man suddenly appeared before him, wearing the half-cloak – the half that Martin had given away! 'Who are you?' Martin gasped, frightened out of his wits. And then he saw that the stranger was Christ himself.

Martin's dream converted him. 'Christ's love has conquered my fears!' he proclaimed. 'I've finished with fighting!'

And he was. Locked away in a dank prison cell, he let his new faith take root and grow. How strong and determined he was when he was finally released. He spent the rest of his life helping the poor and homeless, and spreading the good news of Christ's love.

Eventually, he was made bishop of Tours, but he insisted on living in a tiny hut outside the walls of the great cathedral that was the church building, close to the people he served.

And he served each person he met as if he were serving Christ himself.

GENEVIEVE

(FIFTH CENTURY, FRANCE)

'Only through prayer will the city be saved.'

Genevieve was awakened by another one of her alarming visions.

The savage warrior Attila, king of the Huns – known throughout Europe as the Scourge of God – was marching with his armies toward Paris. On they came, spears poised, shields gleaming, their black hair flying in the wind. Then, before the gates of Paris, Attila and his troops turned south, skirting the city, passing it by altogether.

It was still dark when Genevieve ran into the streets shouting, 'Attila is marching toward Paris! We must fall to our knees in prayer!'

The people cried out in alarm. 'Quickly! Take your children and flee into the countryside!' they shouted as they filled the narrow lanes, running and pushing, blocking the passageways in their frenzy.

'No!' shouted Genevieve. 'Calm yourselves! If we fast and pray, Attila and the Huns will turn south and leave Paris alone! I have seen it in a vision.'

'Ha!' they sneered. 'Crazy Genevieve and her visions! Let her sit here and pray like a good nun. It is she – not us – who vowed to serve God. We will run to safety!'

'Wait!' a man shouted as he climbed on a cart and addressed the crowd. 'Remember when Paris was under siege by the Franks? The city was surrounded; our crops were destroyed; we were all starving. Then Genevieve risked her own life to get food for us. Alone, she went by night up the River Seine and sailed almost one hundred miles to Troyes and brought back boatloads of food.

'Then she pleaded with the king of the Franks for the lives of our soldiers. She went before the executioners, and cried for mercy on behalf of our citizens. So persistent were her cries, the king relented and released them.

'Have you all forgotten so soon? Can you not listen for one moment to Genevieve's pleas? Have you not thought that God may be speaking to us through her?'

The people grew quieter, then shuffled their

feet and looked at each other in silence.

Finally, a woman's voice rang clear and strong. 'I, for one, will answer Genevieve's call to prayer!' she declared.

'So will I!' said another woman from the back of the crowd.

'And I!' shouted another.

Soon a large group of women gathered in the square, fell to their knees and remained there. They refused to eat anything. Genevieve led them, and they began to pray.

They prayed and they prayed.

As the invaders marched closer, the ground shook.

Still the women prayed.

'We're dead!' the guards cried in terror as the army appeared.

But the women kept praying.

And suddenly Attila and all his warriors turned abruptly south, skirting the city. For miles and miles the sound of their heavy feet echoed through the city, until they passed from view and their war calls faded away.

Paris had been spared.

The people stopped laughing at Genevieve. Her reckless courage and devotion to God turned many of them to prayer in times of crisis, and she became so loved and so admired, that she is still remembered today as the defender of Paris.

COLUMBA OF IONA

(SIXTH CENTURY, IRELAND AND SCOTLAND)

'Let everyone live together in love and peace.'

There was blood on Columba's conscience.

He had established numerous monasteries – small communities of men (called monks) who had devoted their lives to serving God. And all over Ireland, his monasteries thrived, proving his passion as a priest. But a priest who had vowed to live in peace should never have been involved in the battle of Cul-drebene.

It happened because Curnan of Connacht had angered Diarmaid, high king over all Ireland, and Diarmaid was hunting him. Frightened for his life, Curnan fled to Columba for refuge, knowing that

within the walls of a monastery those admitted were given sacred protection. No one was ever to violate that rule, not even the high king.

Diarmaid, however, cared nothing about the rules. Late at night his men sprang over the earthen wall, grabbed Curnan and slew him.

'How dare he violate my monastic law!' Columba raged when he heard what had happened. 'Diarmaid must learn a lesson he will never forget.'

Though Columba was a priest, he was also of royal lineage, and the blood of great Celtic warriors pulsed in his veins. The members of his tribe, the Ui Neill, would surely help him: he was, after all, their prince, and Diarmaid their bitter rival who had wrested the throne from Columba's line.

So, with black vengeance in his heart, Columba raised an army from among the Ui Neill and attacked Diarmaid. He won.

But the cost was great: three thousand Celts – young men and women, the flowers of Ireland – were killed, and Columba was responsible. Never had his fiery, impulsive nature caused such harm. Humbled and grief-stricken, he presented himself before the leaders of the church, hoping for mercy. The priests were furious, but in the end they decided not to expel him from the membership of the church. Instead, as penance for his crime, Columba would have to leave Ireland for ever and must labour to bring as many souls to Christ as were killed in the battle of Cul-drebene.

It was a cold, damp day when the warrior-priest and twelve monks tossed their curragh into the Irish Sea. The little basket-boat, nothing more than animal hides stretched tight over a long wicker frame, bobbed and twisted on the waves.

'Now my life will be a pilgrimage for the gospel!' Columba shouted, as he left the shore. 'My place of exile will be the place my curragh lands, for God will be my oars. May the love of Christ heal the wounds of Cul-drebene, and may new life spring up on the thorny battlefield of my soul!'

The curragh bounced and tossed on the waves as it wandered far, first through the North Channel and the Sound of Jura, then west towards the Great Ocean, then north towards the dangerous Sea of the Hebrides.

The clouds blackened, the winds rushed under

the little boat, scooping it into the sky then dropping it hard upon the angry waves, until at last it was tossed against the rocks of a bare, deserted island.

Columba jumped from the boat and ran up on to the island. To the south he saw nothing but white-tipped waves leaping to touch the low, grey sky.

Ireland had disappeared from view.

He spun round to the north and east. 'Here I leave behind my beloved Ireland,' he cried, 'and the spirit of revenge by which I snuffed the light of so many lives! From this new land I will preach only the words of Christ, using nothing but the weapons of prayer, fasting, and ardent devotion to the truth, by which I will fight the dark forces of this world!'

The island was Iona, off the west coast of Scotland. It was stark and fruitless, but there were springs of sweet water and the brothers were used to hard work. Within months, there was a chapel, a kitchen and little stone sleeping huts shaped like beehives. Fields were cultivated and the crops were flourishing; prayers were said day and night; and pilgrims began to visit.

From Iona Columba launched dozens of missionary journeys, spreading Christianity all over Scotland and Northern England. Not only did he win more souls for God than were killed in the battle of Cul-drebene, but entire nations followed Christ because of Columba's influence.

On Iona Columba lived out the rest of his days. His life became a blessing to Christians all over the world, and his dying words still linger in the sea air and in the hearts of all who visit his tiny island: 'Let everyone live together in love and peace.'

A Song for Columba

I cast my small boat upon the sea,
To know where God will carry me;
Oarless, I cannot choose my way;
God is my oar both night and day.

The shore recedes, the waves grow high;
I'm tossed between the sea and sky;
Directionless in my retreat,
God is the one I've come to meet.

No earthen walls, no friends, no kin;
No little hut to seal me in;
My ocean is a desert wide;
I'm shelterless and cannot hide.

I seek God in the ancient tides;
I heed the heavens where God resides;
Within the mist, in Trinity,
I sense God's presence heeding me.

God moves within the darkening sky;
God stirs the depths on which I lie;
God comes to me upon the sea;
God's all around, and breathes on me;

Whose hand is underneath my boat;
Who bears it up, keeps it afloat;
Who marks the place where it will land
And sets me safe where it was planned.

Here on this tiny windswept isle
I make a home in Godly style;
And every day that I am given,
I greet the God of earth and heaven.

I chant in rhythm to the sea;
I sing unto the Mighty Three;
In wind and wave I hear God's voice;
One foot in heaven, I now rejoice.

Here other pilgrims seeking rest
Can pray and worship and be blest;
And with God's Spirit here I'll stay,
Until my Resurrection Day.

BATHILD

(Seventh century, England and France)

'God is my master.'

Bathild lay motionless, crumpled on the ship's deck.

She groaned as snatches of the morning's horrifying events raced through her mind – the weighty net thrown over her head and arms; the sting of the lash; the filthy stench of the pirates; the breath – rank and heavy – of the one who lifted her on board; and finally, her useless, pitiful screams.

The ship pitched and rolled, and England faded from view. Heavy chains bound her ankles; cords secured her wrists. Her eyelids, swollen and sore from crying, fell shut like weighted doors, and she lay there listening to the screech of the gulls until sleep completely defeated her.

When Bathild woke, she was on her back, jostled to and fro. Stars filled a deep, black sky; cartwheels creaked; voices spoke words in the intricate and stylish language of the Franks.

'I am in France,' she groaned in despair, 'sold as a slave.'

Bathild screamed and sat up in bed. It was morning and sunlight streamed through the window of her splendid room high up in the imperial palace. Once again, the old memories had invaded her dreams – but that was a good thing. King Clovis, her husband, had died; and until their son was old enough to rule, Bathild would have to rule in his place. And so she determined never to forget her past.

It was many years since she first arrived at the palace, but the awful events still haunted her. 'Oh Lord, save me!' she had cried when they pulled her from that cart during the middle of the night. The servants removed her chains and tried, with what little English they knew, to make her understand where she was. Then they dragged her in to present her to Erchinoald – the king's mayor and her new master. She straightened her back, looked him directly in the eyes and said, 'I will serve as your slave; but in my heart, where I am always free, I will serve God, Master of heaven and earth.'

In time, because she was so capable and worked so hard, she rose to a high position in Erchinoald's household. And King Clovis, smitten by her beauty and abilities, had asked her to marry him.

In one day, Bathild went from slave to queen.

'And now,' she mused anxiously, shaking herself back to the present, 'I must govern this entire country!

'Lord, help me,' she prayed. 'Show me how I can best serve you.'

She leaped from bed. 'I'm going to the slave markets!' she told her assistants. 'As many as I can, I will set free!'

The terror in the slaves' eyes stirred her heart. She paid the money demanded for them, took them home, fed them and gave them clothes. 'Go now,' she said happily. 'Your ransom is paid! You are free.'

But Bathild's days at the palace were cut short by a group of angry rebels. It was the middle of the night and the shouts outside the palace mingled with her dreams. 'Leave me!' she shrieked, as she sat up, her eyes wide with fear.

Shouts from outside the palace walls: scurrying in the passageway. 'They have come for me,' she breathed in panic.

Her attendants rushed into her chamber. 'Quickly,' they said. 'The rebels are storming the gates. Tell us what to do and we will fight to the death.'

'We will not fight!' Bathild commanded. 'If it is the throne they want, then the throne they can have. But they cannot have me.'

She took nothing with her. All alone beneath bright, welcoming stars in a deep, black sky, she emerged from a secret passageway and walked free.

The humble circumstances of her early life were still a part of her, and she wanted nothing more than to be able to pray, worship and help others. So she walked straight to a monastery for women and became a nun, vowing to live in poverty and to devote the rest of her life to serving the poor in God's name.

And that is exactly what she did.

FRANCIS OF ASSISI

(TWELFTH CENTURY, ITALY)

'The whole creation is my family.'

Francis was so lonely for God, he felt ill.

He had fought as a brave knight, but the killing sickened him. He had worked in his father's shop, selling gold-threaded silks and extravagant French fabrics, but it bored him. Counting coins, drinking and revelling, dancing in fine clothes – such was his life as a rich merchant's son.

Francis ached for riches greater than those of his father's.

For long hours he walked in the beautiful hills near Assisi: how tired and discouraged he was; how he longed to feel the contentment of the birds and the joy of the rushing streams.

One day, filled with despair, Francis fled to the dilapidated church of San Damiano.

'Oh, Lord,' he called, dropping to his knees, 'I yearn for your love and tenderness. What, oh what, would you have me do?'

Deep within his weary, sickened soul, Francis heard a voice. He looked up. The painted crucifix above the altar was speaking to him.

'My church is falling into ruin,' Jesus said. 'I want you to rebuild it.'

Francis leaped to his feet and ran home. Now he knew what to do. His father, Don Pietro, was away, so Francis unlocked the warehouse, took a large roll of dazzling silk damask, and sold it in the market.

Pressing the coins from the sale into the hands of the old priest at San Damiano, he said excitedly, 'Now we can repair the altar!'

When Don Pietro returned, he was furious. He locked Francis in a room.

But Francis' mother secretly unlocked the door and filled his pockets with coins. Back to the old church Francis ran, giving all the gold to the priest. 'We must continue the repairs,' he urged.

In a rage Don Pietro marched to the bishop and demanded that Francis return all his money.

'I will give my father everything I have that belongs to him,' said Francis.

Then, in front of the bishop and everyone there, Francis not only returned the gold but stripped off all his clothes and handed them to Don Pietro.

He stood naked.

'Now I am free!' he proclaimed. 'God's love will be my only wealth.'

Don Pietro never wanted to see his son again.

Francis put on a scratchy brown robe and tied a cord around his waist. He slept on the ground outside the church. He begged for his food, and with his own hands he began rebuilding the crumbling walls of San Damiano.

In time, others joined him. They owned nothing but the robes on their backs. They went into the villages and preached Christ's love. They fed and bathed lepers; they spent long hours in prayer.

Francis was without home and family, but he was not lonely. 'Here is Sister Stream,' he said, 'who gladly quenches my thirst. Brother Air fills me with life, as does God's Spirit. Sister Stars dance with the joy of Christ, Brother Sun warms me with God's love, and Sister Moon lights my darkened path.

'The whole Creation is my family!' he shouted with joy.

Francis preached to birds and fish, wolves and worms, spiders, bees and flowers, because they filled him with an overwhelming sense of God's love.

'Give praise to your Creator!' he told them.

He was the richest man on earth.

ELIZABETH OF PORTUGAL

(THIRTEENTH CENTURY, PORTUGAL)

'We are subjects of the Prince of Peace.'

The July heat penetrated Elizabeth's old bones. She mopped her damp face and fanned her neck, gripping the side of the carriage as it flew along, jolting her aching joints.

Even now the opposing armies would be assembling on the battlefield: the Castilians on one side of the valley, the Portuguese on the other, with her son, Alfonso IV, king of Portugal, calling his men to order.

'Hurry!' she called to the driver. 'The time is short. Alfonso will be stirring up his warriors, giving them the bloodlust.'

Alfonso was an unfaithful son: twice he had led an army of rebels to attack and overthrow his own father, King Denis of Portugal, and twice Elizabeth had intervened and prevented bloodshed.

She was an old woman now, and Denis had been dead many years; but as Portugal's queen, and Alfonso's mother, she would go to the battlefield one last time to fight for peace.

'I fear for you, Madam,' the driver of the carriage called back. 'There will be thousands of men armed with swords and spears.'

'Do not fear for me,' she answered. 'Fear for my son, and the arrows of hatred that have already pierced his heart.'

There was the valley before them: the two armies – bellowing and taunting, spears poised, bows drawn – were ready to strike.

Elizabeth flung herself from the carriage and ran down the empty corridor of ground between the Castilians and the Portuguese.

She stood alone, panting.

'Which one of you will kill me?' she shouted.

There was silence.

'Look at me! I am the face of your enemy! The kingdoms of Portugal and Castile have been fighting each other for generations – and for what? A bit of land, a moment of glory. You are angry, quarrelling cousins, vying for what you think is your birthright. And what do you get instead? Senseless slaughter – the death of your own people for the sake of petty disputes!

'My son, Alfonso, will shed blood rather than talk. But he did not learn this from me! Once you were all young children and your mothers held you on their knees. Their strength was the strength of love. Are you ready to slaughter one of your own mothers? For that is what you must do if you fight this battle – you must kill me first!'

For some time no one moved, then one by one the heavy weapons fell to the ground. Elizabeth's words were from God, and the soldiers – who moments before were ready to kill their neighbours – quietly surrendered to their power and authority. The kings of Portugal and Castile made a truce that day, and there was no war.

There was only one casualty – Elizabeth. Exhausted by heat and fright, she knew her strength was gone, and she died soon after.

Elizabeth the Peacemaker, her people called her after her death. And that is what they still call her today.

BRIDGET OF SWEDEN

(FOURTEENTH CENTURY, SWEDEN)

'I serve the king of heaven.'

Bridget read the summons again.

'King Magnus commands me to serve as lady-in-waiting to his new bride,' she told her husband. 'But I am loath to leave our children and our lands.'

'You forget, Bridget – you are the daughter of the governor of Upland, and a noble lady,' he reminded her. 'Magnus was bound to call you into his service.'

'Magnus! He's weak and foolish. And Queen Blanche is frivolous, feeding on luxury while people in Sweden starve.'

'Then your place is an important one,' her husband replied. 'Magnus and Blanche have much to learn. It is hard for us, yes, but rest assured, God is in this summons.'

'Then God is the one I shall serve,' declared Bridget. 'I will do my best to be a friend to Blanche, but I will not spare the truth.'

Life at the royal court tested Bridget's patience. 'God has blessed you abundantly,' she told Blanche. 'Why not open your hands in generosity and love? Why not serve God in your people?'

But Blanche wanted everything for herself.

Magnus mocked Bridget whenever he saw her. 'Have you received another message from God?' he laughed.

'Yes,' she answered boldly. 'You must put aside your selfishness and do what is right. If you extend your hands in justice, your blessings will multiply!'

But Magnus only scorned her words.

For years Bridget served at the court. She

spoke fearlessly to the royal couple. She taught and prodded and scolded. But they paid no heed.

Finally, she went before the king and said, 'With great patience I have served in your palace. I have been your loyal friend and have spoken God's truth to both you and Blanche, but now I must leave the royal court, for God is not honoured here. As for you, Magnus, I give you one last warning: unless you repent of your wickedness and learn to rule fairly, your power will become as nothing!'

seed for good. You will sow and water, and your efforts will grow into something far greater than yourself.'

But Magnus' heart was shut tight. He and Blanche clung to their lavish comforts, confined in their palace with few friends and few joys.

By now Bridget's husband was dead and her children were grown, so she took the bit of money that Magnus gave her and built a nunnery – a place where women who had vowed to serve God could live and pray together. The nuns were called the Bridgettines; with Bridget, the women tended the sick and gave all their surplus money to the poor.

Bridget's nunnery grew and flourished and became a centre for Christian devotion, study and service. Hundreds more joined the order. Men came too – and in time, the Bridgettines established monasteries and nunneries all over Europe.

When Magnus died, his dazzling wealth meant nothing. The only possession that was truly his was his cold, withered heart – and his reputation as a selfish king. Even to this day, the descendants of his people remember him as the foolish monarch that he was.

When Bridget died, she possessed true abundance. Her years of poverty and service left her surrounded by friends and followers, and her heart was so full of love it spilled over to everyone who heard of her. Then their love flowed to others, and theirs to others, and on and on it went. Through all these centuries her work for the poor has lived on and she is revered the world over as Sweden's patron saint.

These words frightened Magnus and he tried to mend his ways. He knew that Bridget had long wanted to establish a monastery for women, so he gave her a sum of money to start it.

'Surely this money will pay off my debt to God,' the king told himself.

'Foolish, foolish Magnus,' Bridget warned him. 'It is not your money that God wants, but your heart. You serve only yourself, and so your wealth is like diseased fruit withering on the vine. If you serve God, everything you possess will become a

POSTSCRIPTS

Mary

Feast Days: 1 January and 8 September

The divine mystery of Mary's role in the coming of God to earth makes her the most revered of all the saints. When God took on human flesh in the miracle of Jesus' birth, Mary, in humble obedience, mothered her own maker and held in her arms the one who holds the universe.

John the Baptist

Feast Day: 24 June

John was called the greatest man who ever lived because he foretold the coming of the Messiah, then heralded his arrival, pointing to Jesus of Nazareth as the Saviour of the world. When he scolded Herod Antipas for marrying another man's wife, John was imprisoned and eventually beheaded.

Peter

Feast Day: 29 June

Peter's influence was enormous. As the intrepid leader of the early believers at Jerusalem, he performed healing miracles and moved the people to a stronger and deeper faith. He was the first to share Jesus' message with the Gentiles (non-Jews), and was named the first pope of the Roman Catholic Church.

Mary Magdalene

Feast Day: 22 July

For centuries, Christians have looked to Mary Magdalene as their example of a repentant sinner. Delivered from seven demons, she was so devoted to Jesus she risked her own life to remain by his cross as he died, and was granted the honour of being the first person to announce the resurrection of Christ.

Stephen
Feast Day: 26 December

Stephen performed great signs and wonders, was an outstanding preacher and amazed his listeners with his wisdom. Like Jesus, he was falsely accused, tried and killed, and he forgave his murderers. His life and example give strength and hope to those who suffer for their faith.

Paul
Feast Day: 29 June

Paul made three missionary journeys, effectively spreading Christianity all over the known world of his day. Remarkably, his letters of instruction and encouragement to the early believers still exist and are a large part of the Bible's New Testament. Faithful Christians the world over continue to be guided, challenged and inspired by his words.

Laurence
Feast Day: 10 August

Laurence performed miraculous healings, but his examples of love and humility are what make him one of the best-loved saints: he washed the feet of the persecuted, and he fed the starving – even at the cost of his life. According to legend, the Roman executioners roasted him on a gridiron.

Martin of Tours
Feast Day: 11 November

Martin was a miracle worker (some say he even raised a dead man) and lived in extreme poverty as he travelled through the rural villages of France preaching about Christ and destroying pagan temples. The spell of warm weather that often coincides with his feast day is affectionately called St Martin's Summer, in memory of this man who brought new hope to the poor of France.

Genevieve
Feast Day: 3 January

Genevieve's predictions of calamity were numerous, and many were the times when the Parisians, after criticizing her severely, watched as her predictions came true and her prayers brought them relief. People say that even centuries after her death an epidemic of ergot poisoning in Paris ceased when her belongings were carried through the streets.

Columba of Iona
Feast Day: 9 June

During his years on Iona, Columba's reputation as a peacemaker grew, and some people claimed to have seen him in the company of angels while he prayed. He adored books and spent long hours copying them by hand, decorating their pages with illuminating colours and pictures. Several of his books still survive and are some of our finest examples of Celtic art and manuscripts.

Bathild
Feast Day: 30 January

Through her faith in God, Bathild heroically triumphed over her extraordinary circumstances. Her last years were marked by exceptional humility and patience, and her compassion for the helpless has made her the patron saint of children.

Francis of Assisi
Feast Day: 4 October

For Francis, poverty meant freedom to worship Jesus Christ. He so wanted his neighbours to understand the meaning of Jesus' birth that he built the first Christmas crib scene – thus beginning a tradition still practised all over the Christian world; and when he was old, he received the stigmata – wounds in his body that resembled Christ's wounds on the cross. His many followers are called Franciscans.

Elizabeth of Portugal
Feast Day: 4 July

Elizabeth once said, 'If you love peace, all will be well.' Despite an unhappy marriage, and a family torn by rivalry, she planted the seeds of peace wherever she went. Her wondrous gift of reconciliation has led countless people to turn to her during times of war.

Bridget of Sweden
Feast Day: 23 July

Bridget's outspokenness is legendary. She regularly experienced extraordinary visions of Christ's life and of the events of her day, and nothing could stop her from proclaiming the warnings in these revelations – which she did boldly, chiding kings, queens and noblemen, even the pope.